Big Help with my little hands.

Arik-E Hally

This book belongs to:

Author' Desk

It is not by accident that you are the owner of this book.

It is divinely planned.
Before you open more pages, this book is designed to encourage you to be a helper.

There are some activities to engage your mind which require deep thought and the skills page which require you identify the skills of each biblical character.

At the end of each reading you also have some puzzles and drawing to help solidify your learning.

Go ahead and flip open the pages and be deliberate, recording your helpful activities in your activity sheet.

Abimbola Alli (Arike Hally)

Queen of Hide and Seek

- I am definitely my brothers keeper. I am MIRIAM, the sister to two God lovers - Aaron and Moses.

- I am the hide and seek queen, I love watching mum be mum so I can play mum with my dolls and brothers.

- I love to play with my barbie collection and LOL OMG, but I love playing mum with my little brothers the most.

- I run to serve my brother and put a tether- dummy so he stops crying while mum prepares to feed him.

- I joined mum to stop my baby brother from being killed. As the King ask all little boys be killed. The Kings order really made me sad.

- I planned with mum to put baby Mo in the basket while I hid behind the tree to see what happens to him. I played peek-a-boo to keep him calm from afar.

- Hours later, I saw the bling's coming from the Royal maids in their sequinned towels and lot of chatter with praises. I hid properly and prayed someone could help baby Mo.

- Just in time he let out a cry and he was brought before the princess who wondered how she could help baby Mo.

- I stepped out from hiding without being called and gave my suggestion. I was happy as it was the first time of meeting the King's daughter and I spoke boldly just to save my little brother- baby Mo.

- Wow! She listened and asked I act on what I suggested.

- This is the story of how a little me saved baby Mo who became a great man and this made my family very happy.

Think deeply, then write your thoughts

Miriam' Acquired Skills

LIST SOME SKILLS THAT MATCH MIRIAM' ACTIONS.

- [x] Customer/Quality Service
- [ ]
- [ ]
- [ ]
- [ ]
- [ ]
- [ ]
- [ ]
- [ ] Skills Table on last page

Think deeply, then write your thoughts

Prayers

- Dear Lord
- I just read Miriam story of helping her mom, brother and princess.
- Teach me to use the strength you give to me to help others.
- Show me how and tell me when to use my words to help others.
- I thank you for the time when my words and action help others.
- I am your loving little one, who wants to help put a smile on people' face.

Draw any of this scenario on next page.

MY DRAWING

What I learnt from my study

WORD SEARCH

Look for the words listed below.

```
P R I N C E S S M
R S B O E V R S O
A A O T O K R S T
I D A N C E S I H
S L E I H I H S E
E L N T I U E T R
N M O S D C E E U
K R I V E R P R N
B M A I D S I N G
```

Sister   Dance   River   Praise
Brothers Sing   Maid
Mother   Hide   Princess

Date:

My Activities

Fill in what you did during the week in the activity sheet below. How did you help your family and friends each day and how did this make you feel?

SUNDAY	MONDAY	TUESDAY	WEDNESDAY
Today I help	Today I help	Today I help	Today I help
I felt	I felt	I felt	I felt

THURSDAY	FRIDAY	SATURDAY
Today I help	Today I help	Today I help
I felt	I felt	I felt

Helpful activities: Clean the rooms | Find missing items and return them | Read a book and do my homework | Keep my toys away after use

Last Born do Errand

- I am the last born from Jesse clan with 7 handsome brothers.

- I am always absent for the parties. At first, I didn't like this as I like to see beautiful faces and their dressing. I began to accept my reality and go for all errands to ensure guest get the best service as I was regarded as underage at the time.

- I am daddy's boy, he calls me to do everything for him and gives me all I want. I take care of his sheep rearing business and ensured the sheep are protected.

- While on errand, I made singing and music my companion, I do all the dishes singing and have composed many songs while at it. I think I sing more than I shower in the morning.

- My music play and singing was noticed by my neighbours as I sing in church, for children and adults alike. I was recommended to play before the king. Yes! It's like winning gold at the Olympic as I went to the palace to play.

- I have been in fights with animals to protect my father' sheep. These fights made me brave and trust God the more. With my bare hands I tore the lion and bear into pieces.

- Don't overthink it, it was the spirit of God that gave me the strength not little me. This confidence made me fight a big giant that others feared. I won with a stone and a sting for my nation Israel at the battlefront.

- I brought so much joy to my family as we no longer pay taxes on our earnings. And the generous king gave me his daughter as a wife.

- I made friends with the kings son and was dearly loved by him. He protected me from all danger. My friends name is Prince Jonathan – I love him so much and my name is David.

- I am the man who encouraged myself in the Lord when others didn't support me. I am the famous king parents name their children after. I am the loved one, a man after God' own heart.

- Do you think running errands will do you harm?
- Think back on your last chore, what have you learnt to do better?
- When next you are doing chores, what would you be doing alongside your task?
- Do you think David's boldness to fight Goliath was because he fought the animals?
- This story is taken from a Bible book. is the book in the name of a person, town or animal?

Prayers

- Dear Lord,
- I just read a story about David, thank you for giving him strength and faith to do a lot of things.
- Open my eyes to see my area of strength and how I can use this to help others.
- Let me continually use every part of me to praise you.
- Let me listen to you at all times, let my skills be a blessing to my family.
- This I pray loving father in heaven.

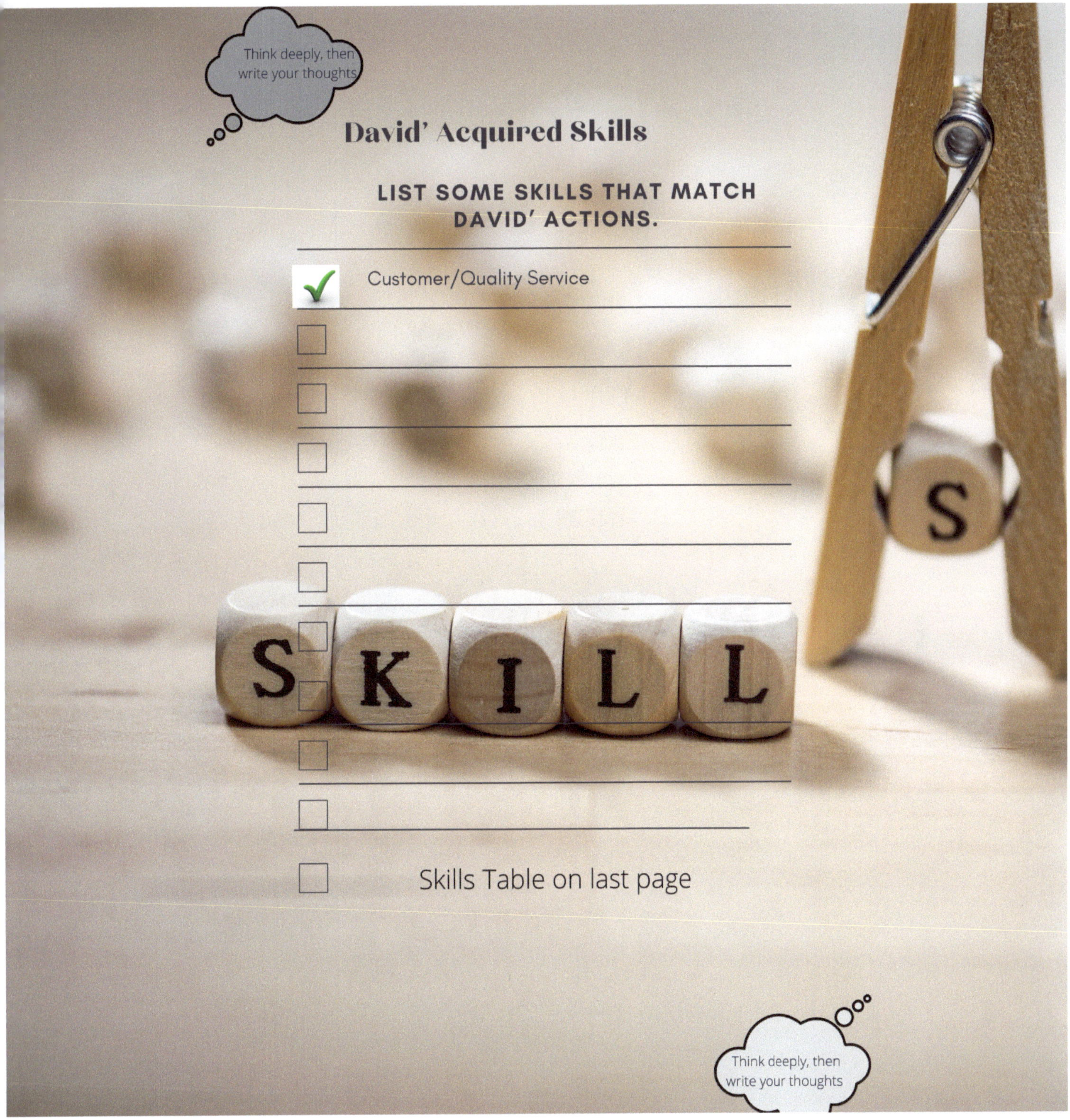

Think deeply, then write your thoughts

David' Acquired Skills

LIST SOME SKILLS THAT MATCH DAVID' ACTIONS.

- [x] Customer/Quality Service
- [ ]
- [ ]
- [ ]
- [ ]
- [ ]
- [ ]
- [ ]
- [ ]
- [ ]
- [ ] Skills Table on last page

Think deeply, then write your thoughts

MY DRAWING

What I learnt from my study

WORD SEARCH
Look for the words listed below.

```
B R O T H E R S F
D S B O E V R E I
E A O T O K I N G
R D V I C K S I H
R L E I D I H G T
A L N A D U E I C
N M U S I C E A U
D N E I R F P N N
I S R A E L I T H
```

Brothers   King   Music   Friend
David   Fight   Sheep
Giant   Errand   Israel

Date:

My Activities

Fill in what you did during the week in the activity sheet below. How did you help your family and friends each day and how did this make you feel?

SUNDAY
Today I help

I felt

MONDAY
Today I help

I felt

TUESDAY
Today I help

I felt

WEDNESDAY
Today I help

I felt

THURSDAY
Today I help

I felt

FRIDAY
Today I help

I felt

SATURDAY
Today I help

I felt

Helpful activities | Clean the rooms | Find missing items and return them | Read a book and do my homework | Keep my toys away after use

Boys can Cook

- We are IsaRebeccah twin boys born the same day but came out at different times.
- We have little or nothing in common except food. We love cooking and eating, that the buffet chefs come for classes.
- Our parents don't condole laziness or assign household responsibility to our maids. We do all the house work, have always wondered what the maids are paid for.
- Dad and mum had their favourite it was obvious. We mentioned this to them as we didn't like it, they tried to change at least we saw some improvement.
- I am a skilled hunter and my twin is a home boy- does majority of the housework before I join him after hunting.
- One day, I was very hungry after a long hunt, thought I would die and was ready to say Yes to anyone.
- Then the aroma of egusi soup drew me closer till I saw my twin and asked for his meal in exchange for anything.
- Smart brother asked for my inheritance- I didn't think he would take it seriously so I agreed to the exchange. That's how he took all that could have been mine. I was angry a long time, but I forgave him later.
- When we finish cooking we would serve our parents and receive their blessings, we don't joke with the blessing no matter how short or long it was, we sealed it with an Amen.
- My twin outsmart me again and took all the blessing my dad was supposed to give me after dressing up like me and serving dad my signature dish (vegetables soup with swallow). This was the last of the blessing dad as he was about to die.
- I was very hurt, and it took years to forgive him, but I got there in the end.
- My name is Esau, and my twin brother is Jacob changed his name to Israel as was told by God. Believe me when I say boys can cook, we can do all we set our hearts to do.

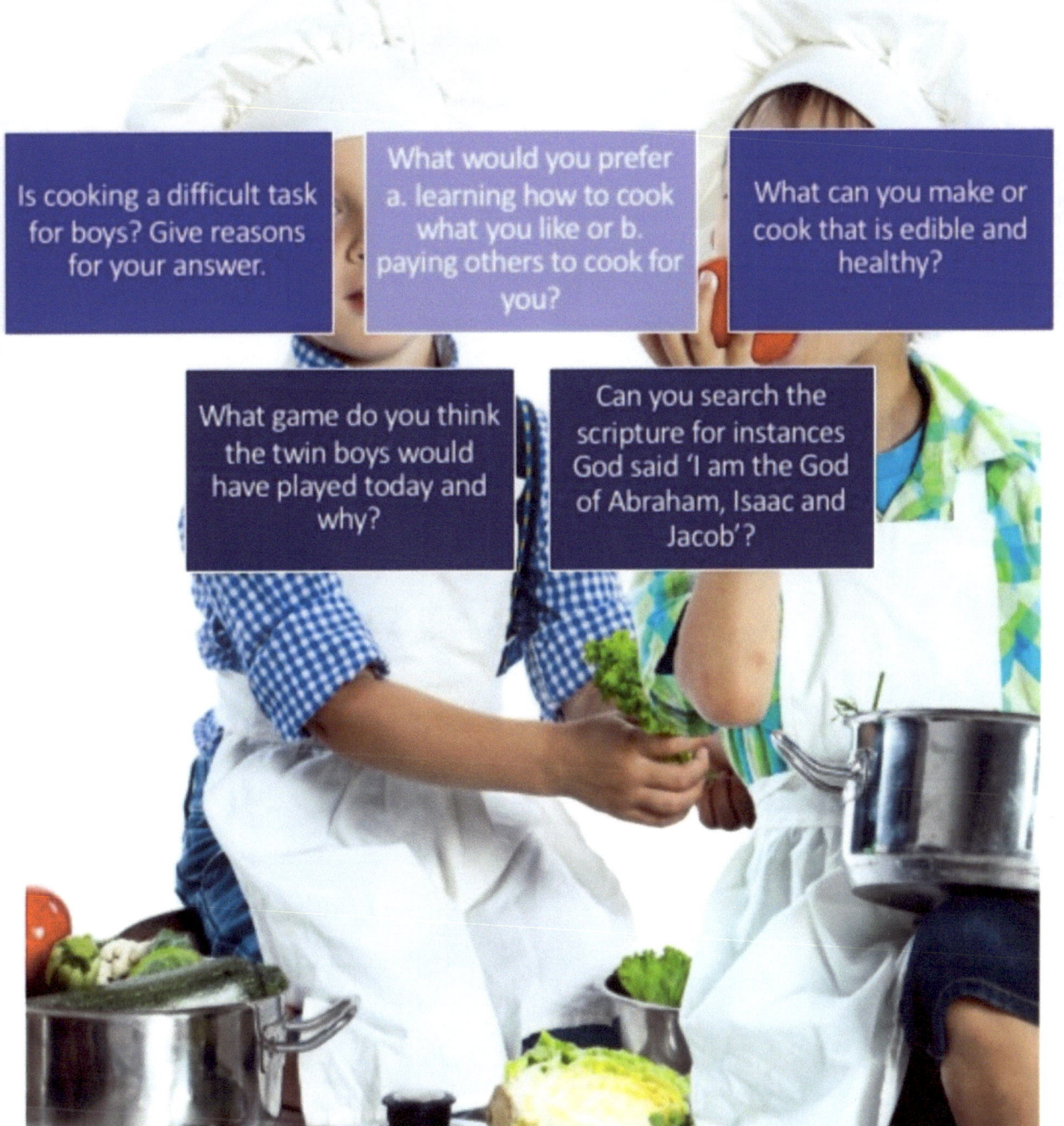

- Is cooking a difficult task for boys? Give reasons for your answer.
- What would you prefer a. learning how to cook what you like or b. paying others to cook for you?
- What can you make or cook that is edible and healthy?
- What game do you think the twin boys would have played today and why?
- Can you search the scripture for instances God said 'I am the God of Abraham, Isaac and Jacob'?

Jacob & Esau' Acquired Skills

LIST SOME SKILLS THAT MATCH TWINS' ACTIONS.

- ✓ Customer/Quality Service
- ☐
- ☐
- ☐
- ☐
- ☐
- ☐
- ☐
- ☐ Skills Table on last page

Think deeply, then write your thoughts

Prayers

- Dear Lord,
- I just read about Jacob and Esau, thank you for making them good cooks.
- Help me to learn to be content with all that I have.
- Let me understand better how you want me to be of service to my parents/guardian.
- When the time is right, let me not be lazy, let me be able to do house chores easily.
- Let me always remember to say Amen when my parents or guardian bless me.

Draw any of this scenario on the next page.

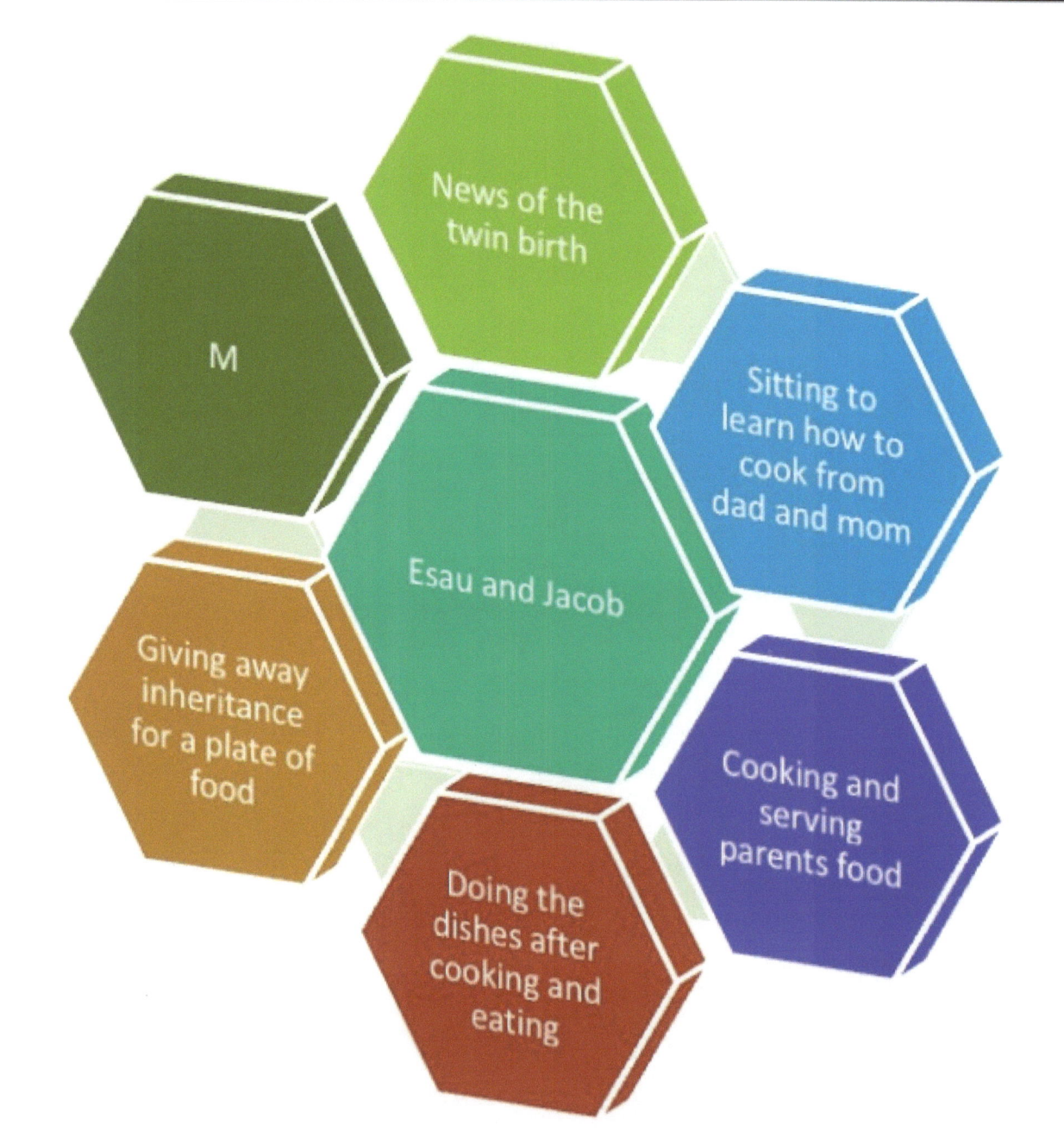

MY DRAWING

What I learnt from my study

WORD SEARCH
Look for the words listed below.

```
J R C N F E S S I
A S B O E V R E S
C A O T O K I S A
O D A N C K S I A
B L E S S I N G C
E L N A I T W I N
N M U S D C N E U
E S A U E R P U N
I S R A E L I N H
```

Twin   Serve   Blessing   Isaac
Jacob   Food   Hunt
Esau   Cook   Israel

Date:

My Activities

Fill in what you did during the week in the activity sheet below. How did you help your family and friends each day and how did this make you feel?

SUNDAY	MONDAY	TUESDAY	WEDNESDAY
Today I help	Today I help	Today I help	Today I help
I felt	I felt	I felt	I felt

THURSDAY	FRIDAY	SATURDAY
Today I help	Today I help	Today I help
I felt	I felt	I felt

Helpful activities: Clean the rooms | Find missing items and return them | Read a book and do my homework | Keep my toys away after use

Skills Table
Match skills below to each character

LEADERSHIP	FRIENDLY/ APPROACHABLE	DETERMINED	ASK FOR HELP	COLLABORATION/ PARTNERSHIP
PERSUASIVE	ADAPTABLE	COMMITTED	EMPATHY	RESPECTFUL
TEAM WORKING	FLEXIBLE	COMPETITIVE	MAINTAIN RECORDS	PATIENCE
HANDLING INFORMATION	CUSTOMER SERVICE	NEGOTIATION	WORKING UNDER PREASURE	RESPONSIBLE
PROBLEM SOLVING	SUPPORTIVE/ HELPFUL	ACTIVE LISTENING	COMMUNICATION	ASSERTIVE

WELL DONE

Always remember, your little hands can do mighty things.

Keep using it for the good of all.

Big Help with my little hands.

Arik-E Hally

www.ingramcontent.com/pod-product-compliance
Lightning Source LLC
Chambersburg PA
CBHW040022130526
44590CB00036B/61